The Texas Rangers: The History and Legacy of the West's Most Famous Law Enforcement Agency

By Charles River Editors

The badge of the Texas Rangers

About Charles River Editors

Charles River Editors is a boutique digital publishing company, specializing in bringing history back to life with educational and engaging books on a wide range of topics. Keep up to date with our new and free offerings with this 5 second sign up on our weekly mailing list, and visit Our Kindle Author Page to see other recently published Kindle titles.

We make these books for you and always want to know our readers' opinions, so we encourage you to leave reviews and look forward to publishing new and exciting titles each week.

Introduction

The Texas Rangers

In the second decade of the 18th century, the precarious state of America's transatlantic relationships began to stabilize. The War of 1812 ended, and the border status with Canada grew somewhat more settled. Turning its efforts toward the taming of an unwelcoming West, the young country faced new and less well-understood enemies. These included a vast array of indigenous Native American tribes, a general lawlessness roaming free from an absence of social protections, and Mexico's historical claims on a large swath of the westernmost portions of the continent.

The contested ownership of Texas produced hostility over the following decades in what is now the 28th American state. The threat of relocating the border with Mexico far to the south at the Rio Grande River was seen as an American land grab of enormous proportions. The Comanche and other large tribes of the region, forced out by farmed acreage and barbed wire fence, viewed the onslaught of American settlement in much the same way. Within these cultural and legal collisions, an outlaw culture took advantage of the structural void. The creation of the Texas Rangers as a response to Indian retaliations and renegade assaults on the banking and transportation systems was born of a need to react quickly. Special skills were required, and unlike the military, resourcefulness and improvisatory thinking were prized alongside obedience to orders. Author Mike Cox described the ideal Texas Ranger as one who is "able to handle any situation without definite instruction from his commanding officer."

It is this resourcefulness, a colorful and non-conformist personality, and a sense of vigilantism that has lent the Texas Rangers a special charisma since their formation. From 19th-century newspaper articles and short stories through early films, the legend of this paramilitary organization has never been without a willing audience. *The Ranger's Bride* was released in 1901, followed by *The Border Ranger* and *The Ranger and His Horse* over the next four years. Radio of the 1940s created a sensation with its treatment of the old Lone Ranger story. The tale continued to bloom in television with Clayton Moore and Jay Silverheels as the Ranger and his companion, Tonto. Karate champion Chuck Norris continued the trend with his serial titled *Walker, Texas Ranger*, employing the name of a famous figure from the Rangers' early years. Uniformly idealized, the true nature of the organization could not be accurately captured by entertainment media. The behavior of the famed citizen protectors fluctuated consistently through their almost two-century existence, complete with tales of heroism and a string of atrocities committed against the innocent.

The Texas Rangers: The History and Legacy of the West's Most Famous Law Enforcement Agency chronicles the remarkable story of the Rangers and their place in fact, legend, and lore. Along with pictures depicting important people, places, and events, you will learn about the Texas Rangers like never before.

Tejas

"All (former Spanish colonies) are now in insurrection. What kind of government will they establish? How much liberty can they bear without intoxication? Are their chiefs sufficiently enlightened to form a well-guarded government, and their people to watch their chiefs? Have they mind enough to place their domesticated Indians on a footing with the whites?" – Thomas Jefferson to Alexander von Humboldt in April 1811

The European explorers who followed in the footsteps of Columbus dreamed of cities made of gold, fantastic creatures and wonders of the Far East. In the mid-1700s there were still expeditions in search of El Dorado, the mythical golden city, to the extent that it was only at the beginning of the 19th century that the Prussian explorer Alexander von Humboldt undertook a real scientific exploration of the new continent, starting with Mexico. Von Humboldt, a naturalist fascinated with every aspect of the exotic landscapes he encountered, was the first to describe current Latin America in precise terms. He drew the most reliable maps, measured the depth of the waters of Mexican ports, and calculated the mineral wealth of its gold and silver mines. Before returning to Europe in 1804, he made a memorable stop in Philadelphia, where he met President Thomas Jefferson. Both were men of science interested in the continent, although for different reasons. From that encounter emerged an intellectual relationship that continued over the years.

Six years later, the War of Independence in Mexico broke out. Led by a priest named Miguel Hidalgo, the United States began observing with interest the developments south of the border. Jefferson had retired from the presidency about a year earlier and devoted himself to reading, building his valuable library, founding the University of Virginia, and holding correspondence with his friends.

One of the most fruitful and interesting exchanges was with Humboldt. In 1811, aware of the bloody and destructive War of Independence in Mexico, Jefferson wrote to the Prussian explorer, "I think it most fortunate that your travels in those countries were so timed as to make them known to the world in the moment they were about to become actors on its stage. That they will throw off their European dependence I have no doubt; but in what kind of government their revolution will end I am not so certain. History, I believe, furnishes no example of a priest-ridden people maintaining a free civil government. This marks the lowest grade of ignorance, of which their civil as well as religious leaders will always avail themselves for their own purposes. The vicinity of New Spain to the United States, and their consequent intercourse, may furnish schools for the higher, and example for the lower classes of their citizens."

Jefferson

Alexander von Humboldt

Jefferson was covertly expressing a widespread belief prevalent at the time in the United States: that Mexicans were an ignorant, inferior race that had to be taught how to govern themselves. The maps and precise geographical observations of von Humboldt would be vital a few years later to the success of the American invasion of Texas and then the whole of Mexico, but Jefferson's letter also revealed a peculiar agitation that ran across the country: if mighty Spain was ready to withdraw from the south, new challenges and opportunities would be presented for the United States.

With the imminent fall of Spanish rule in America, other European countries also began to covet the vast and uninhabited territories of northern Mexico. Although the Mexican rebels were wiped out by the Spanish army, in 1821 the criollos¹ organized a coup d'état against their parents´ country and declared independence from the New Spain. Mexico´s first ruler was an emperor called Agustin de Iturbide, and a map of his domains would have aroused the envy of Alexander the Great: from Panama in the south to Oregon, almost 5,000 miles from border to border, larger than Alexander´s empire. However, the only thing that was impressive about the Mexican empire was its size, as many territories were unoccupied and belonged to it only by name. Most of the population lived in the south and the porous northern border was more a mirage than a reality. In 1821 Mexico possessed about 3 million square miles for just 6 million inhabitants, but in the Empire of Agustin I, the political, economic and cultural life thrived around the capital, Mexico City.

Agustin de Iturbide

In the vast plains, canyons, mountains and lakes that separated Mexico and the United States lived some adventurers, and there were a few missions that Spanish evangelizers had abandoned years ago. Many names that still remain in the southern United States reveal the presence of the conquistadors; San Antonio, El Paso, Victoria, Refugio, and Santa Fe, all of which are Spanish names.[ii]

Texas' original name was "New Kingdom of Philippines, Province of Texas." The name of New Philippines fell into disuse, and around 1800 it could only be found in some official documents. Emperor Agustin de Iturbide was concerned about Texas, "for the abandon with which the previous government (Spain) looked at that interesting point of the empire." But almost none of the six million people in Mexico wanted to move to Texas, even though the government was offering help to families that agreed to colonize the north. Its population didn´t exceed 3,500 Mexican people, concentrated in the towns of San Antonio de Bexar and the Bay of the Holy Spirit (now Goliad). The capital of Texas was Saltillo, nearly 300 miles away to the south, separated by deserts and rugged mountains.

There were good reasons not to move to Tejas, especially since the region had not only the Apache but also the Comanche, Wichita, Caddo, Tonkawas, Cherokees and Karankawa Indians, nations that the Spanish conquistadors had been unable to subjugate. The groups had fierce warriors well stocked with horses and weapons, and in 1835 the Mexican government intensified hostilities, offering 100 pesos for the scalp of every Apache above 14 years old, 50 pesos for each woman's scalp, and 25 pesos per child.

In 1820, a year before Mexico signed its Declaration of Independence, the government began to promote more settlements in Texas and to check the Apache advances. To that end, it granted some lands to Moses Austin to move in with 300 families. Austin had been born in Connecticut and had spent his life starting businesses that ended in bankruptcy, therefore fleeing from one state to another to avoid falling in prison. When he lost everything in a failed banking project, he asked the New Spain for help and swore allegiance in order to be allowed into Texas. He could not capitalize on the generous concession of land because a few months later he died of pneumonia while he was organizing the transfer of the people today known as "The Old Three Hundred."

Thus, it would be his son Stephen, a 24-year-old law student, who would continue the enterprise, at first reluctantly, but finally convinced by a letter from his mother. Stephen Austin presented himself in San Antonio before the governor of Texas, Antonio Martinez, in August 1821. Martinez gave him permission to explore the land and find a suitable location for his colony. Accompanied by some friends and a few Indian guides, Austin headed to the Gulf Coast.

Moses Austin

Stephen Austin

Mexico granted 4,600 acres of land to each family at a cost of $30, to be paid in six years, a real bargain. The land was tax-exempted, and the Mexicans gave them freedom to import whatever they needed from the United States without passing through customs. Most settlers, known as empresarios, arrived with slaves. One of them, a man named Jared Groce, owned over 90.

Encouraged by his initial success, Austin obtained permission to bring 300 more families in 1825 and again in 1829. The Mexican government made a condition that all business transactions be done in Spanish, that settlers dedicate themselves to agriculture or livestock, that they be honest people, and that they be Catholic or convert to that religion. As historian Josefina Z. Vazquez put it, "(The Mexican government) gave away the land, granted tax exemption and allowed free import of items needed for the new colony. They were so exceptional conditions that (Secretary of State) Henry Clay could not help but exclaim: 'Little interest those Mexicans must have in keeping Texas, for they are giving it away!'" (Vázquez, 1998).

In practical terms, Austin acted as governor of the colony. He had every intention of making it a new promised land and to attract hard-working and honest men. He actively promoted it in the United States, tried to pacify the Indians, and managed to arouse the interest of many people. To avoid problems, he decided to handpick the applicants; those accepted were usually people better off than the average, and were literate. Austin established the families away from Mexican settlements, between the Brazos and the Colorado Rivers, and although for years he tried to keep good relationships with his new country, he showed no intention to assimilate into Mexican culture.

Some historians have opined that the demographic profile of the early settlers — literate, wealthier, Protestant men, with capitalist spirit and fervent believers of personal freedom — was crucial to unite them around a common cause. They were also "unkempt and unruly." Historian Gary Clayton Anderson wrote that compared to the other two ethnic groups coexisting with them (the Indians and the Mexicans), "the newly arriving Anglos possessed the clearest sense of identity, which gave them an advantage in the quest for the control of land."

During the 1820s Mexico continued to allow the entry of whites to Texas, under the condition that they swore allegiance to the country and possessed no slaves. However, in opening its borders, Mexico was letting the Trojan horse in, and by 1830 the number of Anglo Texians tripled those of Mexican Tejanos. Even more numerous were the Indians surrounding the area. Although tensions between the three groups were probably unavoidable, Tejanos and Indians were not the most bellicose. According to Anderson, who won a Pulitzer Prize for his book about the conquest of Texas, "One of the shortfalls of most Texas history is the belief that some sense of commonality existed between these three cultures, that the story of Texas is a simple one in which Indians fought Texans and Mexicans quietly receded into the background. In reality, the history of early Texas is characterized by dramatic (...) conflict. The diversity of peoples created anxiety and insecurity, which led to violence among the Anglo, Indian and Tejano cultural groups...Texans mostly blamed Indians for the violence —an unfair indictment, since a series of terrible droughts had virtually incapacitated the Plains Indians, making them incapable of extended warfare." (Anderson, 2005).

Some intellectuals in the Mexican capital began to raise an alarm about the conditions created by the colonization policy. Anglo settlers were rebellious and quarrelsome. Their leaders were far from identifying themselves as Mexican and allowed access to a flood of people, bypassing the quotas authorized by Mexico. Worse still, some people like empresarios David Burnet and Joseph Vehlein began to speculate with lands, selling them on the stock market in New York and Boston rather than transferring them to families as they had promised.

Mexicans, now a minority, began to be treated as inferior beings. Historian David J. Weber notes that "the meeting of Anglo Americans and Mexicans on the Mexican frontier during (the 1820s) contributed to shaping stereotypes in Mexico and the United States which made war between the two nations nearly unavoidable by 1846." "They called them Spaniards or greasers," adds Mexican writer Jose Emilio Pacheco, "because to the Anglo-Saxon look, their dark skin seemed to be the effect of dirt and because they cooked their food with fat" (Pacheco, 1997).

Most historians have ignored this sensitive aspect of the first generations of Texians because it would portray them as racist and the war itself as an openly though not exclusively racist movement. Texians feared "the pollution of (the Texians') wives and daughters by the Mexican soldiers. Some whites were already regarding Mexicans (…) to be considered less than human and this dispensable, like Indians, Africans and animals. Creed Taylor recalled: 'I thought I could shoot Mexicans as well as I could shoot Indians, or deer, or turkey, and so I rode away to a war.'" (De Leon, 1983).

Finally, there was the question of slavery. Many Americans, burdened with debts, affected by the agricultural crisis in the Mississippi Valley, and fleeing debtors, began arriving in Texas with their slaves. In 1826 Austin was overseeing 1,800 people, about a quarter of them black slaves. Since Mexico didn't allow slavery, "the immigrants took the precaution of signing indenture contracts with their illiterate servants binding them for ninety-nine years to work off their purchase price, upkeep, and transportation to Texas."

In only three years the Anglo population increased to 8,000 people, most of them admitted with generous land grants. However, in 1830 the president of Mexico, Vicente Guerrero, the first African-American president of the Americas, abolished slavery once and for all. Although Texas was temporarily exempted from the measure, the news alarmed the owners of that northern territory since almost all settlers had slaves (Vazquez, 1998). Texians had fiercely resisted assimilation; although the grace period was over, they refused to pay taxes and tariffs, and began to conspire. In the capital of Mexico, it was no longer a secret that something was cooking.

Forming the Rangers

In 1823, Mexico announced that it would dedicate no resources to Tejas, or supply any means of protection. The subsequent creation of a home-grown, albeit undefinable body of protectors, easily disbanded once called into service, was the perfect political response. The first era of Texas Rangers would be manned by "citizen soldiers," well before the installation of professional lawmen. However, in fulfilling his responsibilities to the original settlement, Austin not only forged a legend as the "Father of Texas," but of the agency that so successfully protected the future republic.

Even as tensions brewed, Austin's town and localized militia served another of Mexico's purposes: to serve as a buffer against Comanche raids. Through much of the early 19th century, the Comancheria Empire thrived through present-day Texas to the far American Southwest. Owning most of the horses in the region, the vast tribe obtained much of its supplies through raids against the Spanish, Mexican, and American outposts on its borders. Of primary concern were settlements at San Antonio de Bexar and Laredo. The Tonkawa, Karankawa, and southern Apache tribes comprised much of the indigenous populations of the region as well.

Austin's continued efforts to forge a workable plan with the Mexican government faltered, at one point landing him in a Mexican prison. Moses Morrison, his right-hand man, took control of the early Rangers until Austin's return, and the new force set about patrolling the expanse, capturing notorious criminals and resisting native incursions. Morrison, a North Carolinian, was among the 'Old Three Hundred' and an army veteran. As Austin's 1st Lieutenant, he led the first Ranger mission in that year. His force of ten men was sent to the Colorado and Tres Palacios Rivers to control a group of Karankawa raiding white settlements. Following his return, Austin put out a call for ten additional men "to act as Rangers for the common defense."[1] Wages were set at $15 per month, generally payable in guaranteed tracts of land.

Not yet known as the Texas Rangers, the small group filled an immediate need and caught the fascination of those who enjoyed their protection. According to the descriptions offered by the Bullock Museum of Texas, the first Rangers were "a raggedy bunch, [but] they polished up right nicely."[2] More analytical comparisons likened them to the most "colorful, efficient, and deadly band of irregular partisans"[3] the world of law and order has ever seen. The Tejas militia, also described as Rangers, is considered the precursor to the official force, despite operating under numerous names.

In the two years following the Mexican War of Independence from Spain and the first white settlers' relocation to Texas, 700 new families followed. Including the era of early Rangers in the force's chronology makes them the second oldest law enforcement agency with a statewide jurisdiction in the United States. Through the years, despite amassing smaller numbers than its fellow agencies, the Rangers have been favorably compared to the FBI, Scotland Yard, Interpol, and the Royal Canadian Mounted Police. Among modern researchers, some find a significant connection to the RCMP, establishing order through the removal of Indians from their land, tightly controlling all ethnic and mixed blood societies, assisting the prospects of large ranchers over the fortunes of smaller ones, and anti-union work. Such a connection is not altogether surprising, as the Ranger format was taken directly from a British model and embedded into American military life. Britain produced numerous examples of guerilla Ranger organizations throughout the continent in the 18th century. In a style contrary to the image of a Texas cowboy on horseback, several of the early companies fought on foot. In the mold of their British ancestors, they even employed a fife and drumming corps. Where these props of war may have intimidated European opponents, the Comanche and Apache were unmoved, rendering the psychological effects useless. Transforming their fighting style to that of frontier cavalrymen employing the tactics of trained horsemen resulted in far greater success.

In order to thrive as an ongoing unit, the idea of a corps of Rangers required an "implacable foe."[4] In a rich environment for conflict, the Rangers found several, from "unyielding Mexicans

---

[1] Mike Cox

[2] Bullock Museum, Texas Rangers – www.TheStoryofTexas.com/discover/campfire-stories/texas-rangers

[3] Bullock Museum

[4] Harold Weiss, Jr., The Texas Rangers Revisited: Old Themes and New Viewpoints, the *Southwestern Historical Quarterly*, Vol. 97 No. 4 (Apr, 1994), pp620624

[to] indomitable Apaches,"[5] among others. Critics are quick to mention that Austin's Rangers did not arise out of the military so much as private companies. The suggestion is rampant in some quarters that the corps was "born of vigilantism"[6] and aptly proved it in numerous instances of bloody combat. They add that few captains of the Rangers came from their own ranks in the early years and that their usefulness was sporadic before the Civil War.

Some believe that the corps' search-and-destroy style missions, drawn from English and Scottish traditions, added to the erosion of their discipline and collective ethics. Allied only through mercenary exchanges and Texan pride, Austin's men "fought under no flag, wore no uniforms, [with] no prescribed length of service."[7] Working on an "as needed" basis, the rules and guidelines for service were loosely incomplete. Some Rangers served for a matter of days, while others were on duty for months at a time. Members of the local population knew their protectors under a variety of names, including "ranging companies, mounted gunmen, mounted volunteers, minutemen, spies, scouts, [and] mounted rifle companies."[8]

Whatever their reputation, in the immediate circumstances surrounding Tejas during the early 19th century, the Rangers proved to be the least expensive method for resisting native incursions. Apart from combat, they served the national military as scouts to worldwide acclaim. In addition to protecting a Mexican province headed for war due to its changing makeup, Rangers became invaluable scouts in the western exploration of the continent. In 1830, they scouted and mapped the most effective route for the U.S. Army to travel from the coastal Brazoria to Monterrey, California via Jenning's Crossing on the Colorado.

The official Texas Rangers were established on October 17, 1835, although the name took some time to catch on. The plan for establishing a free-roaming law enforcement entity was proposed at the "Consultation" on that date by Daniel Parker. A transplanted Virginian, Parker was a Baptist leader in the South and helped to establish the church in Texas. Representing Nacogdoches County at the General Council, the proposal was adopted, a bold step considering the reality of Mexican rule.

A month after the Consultation, Robert McAlpin Williamson was chosen as the first member of the corps, which began with 50-60 men divided into three companies. Williamson, a passionate proponent for self-rule in a Texas Republic and attendee of the Consultation, had served in combat with the cavalry. As the first officially instituted Ranger, he made for an auspicious beginning as a gifted legal mind who later became a Supreme Court Justice for the breakaway province. Williamson was a victim of tubercular arthritis, known at the time as "white welling,"[9] a condition that caused his right leg to freeze at a 90 degree angle. Throughout his

---

[5] Harold Weiss, Jr.

[6] Harold Weiss, Jr.

[7] Harold Weiss, Jr.

[8] Mike Cox

[9] Biographical Encyclopedia of Texas, R.M. Williamson entry – www.georgetown.-texas.org/WILLIAMSON_ROBERT_M__Three-legged-

career, Williamson was affectionately dubbed "Three-Legged Willie."

Williamson

Among the charter members of Austin's Rangers was John J. Tumlinson, a North Carolinian who arrived in Texas as a member of one of the first settler families. He had traveled throughout the area two years prior at the age of 17, during which time his father was killed in an Indian attack. With his brother and a recruited group of friends, he tracked and killed each perpetrator, one by one. Such was the type of personality most highly sought by Austin for his vision of frontiersmen protectors. In the year of the Consultation, Tumlinson was made a 1st Lieutenant in the company led by Robert M. Coleman, having fought in the Battle of Gonzales two weeks before Parker's proposal was carried.

The brief battle was not a conflict of major significance in tactical terms, but it served as one of the strongest political signals that a revolution would soon break out against Mexico on behalf of a new Texas Republic. Mexico had offered the community one cannon for protection, but with changing attitudes, the Mexicans felt it unwise to leave such a weapon in the possession of a potential enemy. A return of the cannon was requested, and when the town refused, 100 Mexican dragoons appeared to seize it. Townspeople stalled the soldiers while reinforcements came from neighboring communities. Eventually, 140 Texians appeared and approached the Mexican camp. Opening fire, the Mexican contingent soon thought better of the idea and withdrew. Of the major figures in the Gonzalez action, William W. Arrington became one of the "Immortal Eighteen" who refused the demands of Santa Anna's brother-in-law, General de Cos. He also served on a committee of 12 to draw up the provisional government for the future Republic.

Santa Anna, best known for attacking the Alamo, assumed leadership over the Mexican government after overthrowing the national constitution and taking a hard line against the Texas settlements. Upon receiving news from Gonzales, he sent General Martin Perfecto de Cos to San Antonio with reinforcements. Still in early October, the arriving Mexican troops lay siege to the town. Strong enough to hold out for a lengthy period, soldiers and settlers of San Antonio were prepared for such an eventuality. However, as the stalemate wore on, morale plummeted on both sides. Isaac Burleson of the Rangers proposed a troop withdrawal, but was overruled by his officers. Ironically, the Mexicans occupied the Alamo, where many of the San Antonio defenders would later perish. Although a token surrender was eventually signed on the part of the Texians, it was the Mexicans who agreed to leave after a period of six days. No interactions were allowed with Texians during that time if any party carried weapons. Historians describe the longest campaign of the revolution as one of the only major Texas victories. Following his commission as a Ranger officer, Tumlinson took a company of 60 men to establish Fort Tumlinson and to Bushy Creek in order to protect Anglo-American settlements there. Upon hearing that Santa Anna was invading, the post was abandoned and later burned by Indians in the region. Devoting his life to fighting Mexicans and marauding tribes, Tumlinson suffered loss after loss, including his brother Andrew, as well as his wife and son.

Antonio Lopez de Santa Anna

Over the following two years, Ranger numbers increased to over 300 and included such luminaries as Ben McCulloch, who had followed family friend Davy Crockett to Texas in the previous year. McCulloch would go on to a valorous career in actions against Native American tribes, and he participated as a central figure in the Texas Revolution as a 1st Lieutenant under Jack Coffee Hays. Only an onset of measles prevented him from joining Crockett at the Alamo, where all defenders lost their lives in February and March of 1836.

Ben McCulloch

The size of the Ranger force fluctuated throughout its existence, based on the available funding, which was often scarce. Wages promised were not always delivered, and each Ranger was responsible for his own clothing, firearms, and horse. Badges were only occasionally worn, but a standardization of the badge or uniform was still decades away during Austin's leadership. The star badge that would come to be associated with the Texas Rangers was forged from a Mexican Cinco Peso coin and was worn by a few of the early members. It was almost a certainty that when the Rangers went out to confront a criminal situation, they were vastly outnumbered. However, through their skills and attention to the latest developments in weaponry, they were almost always able to prevail. At times facing large groups, they carried multiple pistols and a variety of hand-to-hand weapons. For distance shooting, they often carried Tennessee and Kentucky rifles. In the beginning, they shot Spanish pistols that required frequent dismounting to reload.

Although most of the first Rangers hailed from the American South, members also had roots in Ireland, Germany, Scotland, and England and spoke in their native accents. However, their shooting, fighting, and riding skills made them as one. Serving only as sporadically paid "unintended volunteers,"[10] their fame spread quickly. According to one writer of the time, the new corps of Rangers could "ride like a Mexican, shoot like a Tennessean, and fight like the devil."[11] The crisp regimentation of a state or national military force was antithetical to the mission of the improvisatory Rangers. Likewise, the coded niceties of armed conflict, in place for centuries of European warfare, were all but abandoned. As a general rule, the new paramilitary organization "never gave nor asked for quarter."[12]

Early Years

Santa Anna's Mexican Army also provided no quarter during the Texas Revolution in 1836. The Gonzalez Ranging Company of Volunteers remains the only company in Ranger history to be lost entirely, in the massacre at the Alamo. In the aftermath, other Ranger companies worked to protect retreating families in what was termed the "Runaway Scrape." In almost every case in which the fleeing settlers were pursued, few prisoners were taken, with the order of mass executions coming directly from Santa Anna. Rangers participated in virtually every action, including service with the main army under Sam Houston. Despite the brutality, settlers stood firm as rights were violated and emigration was cut off for both men and women. Anecdotes tell of a Gonzalez Ranger's wife cutting and resewing her wedding dress into a Lone Star flag in defiance of Mexican forces. Among the most decisive battles of the revolution in which Rangers took a major part was the Battle of San Jacinto, fought on April 21, 1836, less than two months after the Alamo.

[10] Mike Cox
[11] Mike Cox
[12] Harold J. Weiss, Jr.

Houston

Stephen Austin died on December 27, 1836, but he lived to see the early signs of the establishment of his republic and a significant increase in Ranger numbers. Such growth was essential in the early years as perils to the nascent state occurred exponentially. Austin's structure for the Rangers endured, despite the chaotic environment in which it existed during the continuing revolution. The founder was succeeded by Sam Houston, leader of the Texian army. Under his command, the number of Texas Rangers grew to 300, but they were used sparingly during the following three years. Houston actively pursued peaceful coexistence with all the displaced tribes, including the Cherokee, the home tribe of his wife. Direct collisions subsided, and the Rangers occupied their time serving as scouts and couriers. Not surprisingly, following such a passionate Revolution, most considered their work retrieving cattle, escorting refugees from one place to another, or destroying supplies and equipment left by the Mexican Army as menial and uninspiring.

That said, the new frontier was not entirely quiet, and several individual battles not connected to a larger cause suddenly ignited. In November 1837, a band of Kichai raided Fort Smith on the Little River. With a large group of Rangers, Captain William Eastland chased them for days up the Colorado River, eventually losing the trail. At that point, the upper-level officers began to quarrel, and the company split. A group of 17 Rangers soon picked up the trail again, and a Kichai guide leading a band of Cherokee and Delaware was located and immediately killed.

Those in his party were spared after swearing allegiance to the new Republic. The band of Kichai was found, and a bitter battle ensued, during which Rangers abandoned their horses in a ravine. Hand-to-hand combat went on for two hours, and at one point, the Kichai started a range fire to smoke out the Rangers from their positions. To their surprise, the company of Rangers charged through the fire, and 10 Kichai were killed fleeing. Eight survived and later turned themselves in by walking into a settlement, having lost their horses and equipment.

The year of 1837 also marked the command of Captain John "Jack" Coffee Hays, one of the most successful and feared leaders of the early Rangers. Within three years of his arrival at San Antonio after yellow fever took both parents, he was appointed to the rank of captain at the age of 23. His reputation as a fighter always prepared to abandon caution grew quickly, and men who served under him pointed with pride to their time in Hays's company. Lipan Flacco, an Indian aide who rode with him, often referred to Hays as "Brave too much."[13] Beside his adventurism and tough bravado, Hays kept a close watch on developments in weaponry technology, always sure to arm himself and his men with the best available whenever funding allowed it. From his time in Mississippi, where he joined up with Erastus Deaf Smith and his Rangers in south Texas, Hays seldom skipped a battle. He stopped on his way to Texas only to help bury the dead at the Goliad massacre. More than 500 prisoners of war were executed there under Santa Anna's orders, despite the reluctance of his senior officers. In the following months, he won "three fearsome battles"[14] against the Comanche and acquired the nickname of "Devil Yack Jack."[15] The Comanche referred to him as the "White devil,"[16] while the Mexicans employed the term "Texan devil." His fame expanded when he captured the famous outlaw Juan Sanchez as he hid in a settler's ranch. With a small group of Rangers, Sanchez's band was ambushed, then chased before a gun battle ensued. Eventually, Sanchez was caught and hanged. Soon after, Hays tracked a band of Comanche who had slaughtered a settler family, including two young children. He found them along the Llano River and killed almost all of them.

[13] Mike Cox
[14] Bullock Museum
[15] Bullock Museum
[16] Rino de Stefano, Captain Jack is the Real Tex Willer, La Liguria (June 2002) – www.rinodestefano.com/en/artiles/rangers.php

Hays

The Battle of Bandera Pass was a sore spot within the Texan military, as the Comanche generally held the advantage in weaponry. In 1840, raiding parties under Buffalo Hump attacked the towns of Victoria and Linnville, setting up a confrontation in the pass, a gap in the mountains named for an 18th-century Spanish commander. Hays arrived with the cream of Ranger personnel, all bearing a new weapon: the Paterson Colt five-shot revolver. The precise date of the battle is unknown, but 50 Rangers successfully took on hundreds of Comanche warriors and lost only five men. The new weapon inspired such confidence that when the Comanche retreated, the Rangers followed to take advantage of the turning point.

Through the efforts of John Coffee Hays, the Texas Rangers became one of the first institutional clients of Samuel Colt, a New England gun maker. The .36-caliber five-shot revolver was to be the first of several major weaponry upgrades, some improvements coming at the personal suggestion of Hays himself. In earlier battles, the one-shot pistol not only required constant reloading, but at times protection offered by dismounting and using one's mount as a shield. On the way to perfecting the multiple-shot revolver, Colt made important upgrades during the war with Mexico. By the time the five-shot, described as "fragile,"[17] then the six-shooter came into regular use with a caliber up to .45, Ranger weaponry became the "frontier equivalent of a nuclear bomb."[18]

Colt

Mirabeau B. Lamar became the next President of the Texas Republic in 1838, with a policy in direct contrast with that of Samuel Houston. The idea of peaceful coexistence or even a basic civility toward the tribes of the Republic was abandoned. The Rangers were thrown into a general assault on all non-whites in Texas. Lamar, a Georgian with a passion for Texan independence, was by all accounts an educated and artistic person who came to power in circumstances requiring greater aggression. He was a voracious reader, an excellent horseman and fencer who wrote poetry and painted in oils. Two famous verses remain from his private works, *At Evening on the Banks of the Chattahoochee* and *Thou Idol of My Soul.* However,

---

[17] Mike Cox
[18] Mike Cox

unlike Houston, Lamar had skirmished with the Cherokee and never forgot or forgave what he claimed was their support for the Mexicans in the Cordova Rebellion against the republic. Sensitive as he may have been in other aspects, defeat of the tribes was not enough for Lamar. He supported a policy of total eradication, and was supported in that campaign by Texas Supreme Court Justice Thomas Rusk. In the two years leading up to Lamar's rise, Rusk served as Secretary of War under Houston. Both Rusk and Lamar understood that the best way to pursue their policy of annihilation was to increase the ranks and assignments of the Texas Rangers.

Lamar

As a colonel with battlefield experience, Lamar responded firmly to the situation, as required by the difficult circumstances in which the fledgling republic found itself from the beginning. Following the revolution, Texas still had no treaties with former aggressors, and Mexico would not recognize the republic, threatening to invade again. The ire of the regional tribes was raised once more, and there was no money in the treasury. Due in large part to Ranger efforts, the Cherokee were driven into Arkansas, and a campaign against the Comanche cost well over two million dollars. When Mexico continued to deny the republic's existence, Mirabeau formed an alliance with Yucatan and sent the Texas Navy there.

Hostilities reached a peak on March 19, 1840, when representatives of Texas and the Penataka Comanche nation met to discuss the handing over of abducted prisoners and the status of the tribe within the boundaries of Texas. Under the impression that they attended as ambassadors, the Comanche were represented by Muk-Wah-Ru. Approximately 30 Comanche warriors were in attendance, with five women and children. The Texans, backed up by the Rangers as an enforcement arm, requested that the tribe vacate Texas entirely, a difficult proposition with bands of Cheyenne and Arapaho already raiding their northern borders. Muk-Wa-Ru arrived with a handful of prisoners. An abused and mutilated Matilda Lockhart and her younger sister, prisoners for nearly two years, became pawns in the negotiations, but were not produced until later in the day. The sister had been victimized by 'roasting' torture, and Matilda's appearance when produced by a member of the tribe later that day was ghastly. The appalled Texans opened fire at the meeting, killing all but one, allowing one woman to return home to tell the story. Resisting the Comanche's coming retaliation was left up to an abruptly increased Ranger force. In the following summer, an enormous war party of Comanche rode through the Guadalupe Valley, sacking the community of Linville. Settlers were killed, structures were burned, and large numbers of livestock were stolen. In a constantly moving gunfight, Ben McCulloch and his Rangers came together with the militia and a Tonkawa party against the Comanche under Buffalo Hump. The Rangers pursued the raiding party to Plum Creek on August 11, near present-day Lockhart. They claimed to have killed 80 of the enemy, despite finding only 12 bodies, and recovered much of the livestock. The Comanche might have proven more difficult to catch had it not been for their greed in attempting to steal so many horses and cattle.

Through the next two years, the tribes continued their incursions, in part because they had so few viable alternatives for relocation. More acreage was allotted to farming, symbolized by many miles of barbed wire. At the same time, unrest continued in the Mexican government, and a second invasion remained likely in the eyes of many Texans.

In 1841, Houston was reelected to replace Lamar. This should have served as a good sign for improving relations, but too much blood had been shed. A new law was passed authorizing yet another company of 150 men to "act as Rangers"[19] for the purpose of fending off Mexican incursions in the southern and western portions of the republic. These men were, as before, placed under Hays, perhaps the most forthright commander of any Ranger company in history. However, the tribal invasions also continued, and for all his empathy, Houston could not ignore the situation. The two years preceding had resulted in a record number of battles and casualties. During that time, 33 Texas Rangers were killed and over 50 wounded. In addition to the larger Ranger group, another 20 "minutemen" were authorized with an upgraded regimen of training, rules, and attitude. Formalized training programs were introduced, and admission into the Rangers narrowed to accept a higher quality recruit. Solidifying the identity of the companies, Hays produced an "esprit de corps"[20] unknown to previous manifestations of the on-again, off-again force.

Unlike the Rangers of old, who would serve for months on end as needed, Houston's Rangers were forbidden to serve for more than 15 consecutive days or a total of more than four months. In addition to Hays' company, other units were sent out to face the Comanche under the

---

[19] Legends of America, Texas Legends, the Texas Rangers – Order Out of Chaos – www.legendsofamerica.com/texas-rangers.html
[20] Legends of America

command of Antonio Perez, John T. Price, and John Henry Moore, who had begun a series of raids against the tribes along the Colorado during the previous fall. In one incident, Moore slaughtered the great majority of a large Comanche village, further hardening the enemy's ire against the republic. By 1841, Price and Perez were leading actions in the Cross Timbers and present-day Dallas/Fort Worth areas. The ascension of Hays continued, and to the present day, he is considered to be the individual under whom "the best tradition of the Texas Rangers was established."[21] As a historical figure among the organization itself, Hays is considered to fit the profile of "the ideal Texas Ranger."[22] His recommendations to Samuel Colt for an improved hand weapon had changed the republic's fortunes, not only at the Battle of Bandera Pass, but in many future encounters. With him were commanders "Bigfoot" Wallace, Ben and Henry McCulloch, Samuel Walker, and Robert Addison 'Ad' Gillespie. These men represented the best of the best since the establishment of the Rangers.

[21] Stephen Moore, Savage Frontier, Volume III, 1840-1841 – www.untspress.edu/sites/default/files/excerpt/press270.pdf
[22] Stephen Moore

Walker

William A. A. Wallace, a Virginian, was descended from Scottish highland noblemen William Wallace and Robert the Bruce. When a brother and cousin were killed at Goliad, he set out for Texas to "take the pay out of the Mexicans."[23] Captured during the ill-fated Meier Expedition into Mexico, he was involved in the Perot Prison incident, in which every 10th man to draw a black bean from the bag was to be executed, the others being set free.

Bandera Pass was a gap in a group of mountains near the town named for an earlier Spanish commander from the 18th century. Commander Hays arrived in the morning with approximately

---

[23] Texas Rangers Hall of Fame and Museum, William A.A. Wallace "Big Foot" – www.texasranger.org/halloffame/Wallace_William.htm

50 Rangers and was surprised by a large party of Comanche under Buffalo Hump. The precise date and time are unknown. Hays outfitted every man with a new Colt revolver, a weapon unknown to the Comanche at that time. The battle lasted all day, with 50 Rangers ably holding off hundreds of Comanche warriors. Although the conflicts would rage on for another 34 years, the day in which this technological advantage first appeared is marked as the turning point of the larger conflict.

Wallace

Serving with Bigfoot Wallace was a fellow survivor from the Perot Prison black bean episode, a Marylander named Samuel Walker. Joining Hays' company by 1842, he fought in the Battle of Salado Creek, considered to be the final major battle against invading Mexican troops. He joined Hays' company as a member of the spy company.

In a further upgrade to Samuel Colt's revolver technology, his new black powder repeater was made available, named the Walker Colt in honor of Samuel Walker's service. In 1844, both

Walker and his namesake weapon distinguished themselves at the Battle of Walker Creek. Hays' company chased a large band of Comanche along the Pima Trail and the Guadalupe River. Camping on June 9, one of the Rangers was about to fell a "bee tree" when a band of approaching Comanche were reported. Noah Cheery famously called from atop the tree: "Jerusalem, captain, yonder comes a thousand Indians!"[24] The war party actually consisted of approximately 200 and was led by Yellow Wolf. A group of 20 attempted to lure the rangers into the forest. That failing, the entire force appeared as a show of strength, but the Rangers dismounted and attacked anyway. With the Walker Colt, the battle sent the Comanche retreating, despite the small Ranger numbers. The Comanche lost 50 men, including their chief. Walker was superficially wounded in the conflict.

Walker went on to participate in the Mexican-American War, which began in 1846, leading companies for Zachary Taylor and Winfield Scott in the battles leading up to the taking of Mexico City. These included the Battle of Palo Alto on May 8, 1846 and the Reseca de la Palma on the following day. Palo Alto was noted for the abandonment of bayonet charges in favor of mobile cannons ferried from spot to spot by wagons, a tactic thought to be preposterous at first, but in the end largely effective. The Reseca de la Palma immediately followed, as Taylor caught a retreating Mexican army and inflicted heavy losses, approximately 400 over the two days.

In the Battle of Veracruz during the push into Mexico, Scott's Rangers consisted of five companies, all camped along the Japala Road at Vergara, three miles to the west. By this time, Texas was in the early stage of its incarnation as an American state. That reality caused consternation with President Polk at the truce struck by Scott in Veracruz after the March 17, 1847 battle. For generations, families of Mexican heritage have perceived the march from Veracruz to Mexico City as an offense of historical proportions. Many point to the invasion of Mexico as a U.S. betrayal of its own constitution, "the first aggressive invasion of a sovereign nation."[25] In an instant advantage, Commander Hays armed each Ranger with a new Colt revolver. At that point, the march on Mexico City was begun in earnest. In the Battle of Monterrey, fought in September of 1846, a group of Rangers stormed Federation Hill and captured a contingent of cannons overlooking a "door to door struggle"[26] of fierce fighting. They used these cannons to bombard retreating Mexican troops. As General Pedro de Ampudia realized that his army was caught in a growing disadvantage, he called for a truce, which was granted. Samuel Walker was wounded in the assault on the Bishop's Palace, on the highest point in Monterrey. Following the battle, President Polk and General Scott formulated the plan of attack, a direct assault on Mexico's primary city.

Companies of Rangers distinguished themselves at the Battle of Cerro Gordo on April 18,

[24] Texas Ranger Hall of Fame and Museum
[25] Jeffery Robenalt, Diablos Tejanos: The Texas Rangers and the Road to Mexico City – www.texasescapes.com/Jeffeery/Robenalt/Diablos-Tejanos/htm
[26] Texas Ranger Hall of Fame and Museum

1847, generally considered the first major engagement in the Mexican-American War. The conflict pitted Taylor against Arista Mariano. Thanks to modern weaponry and other factors, the Mexican forces lost over 400 men and the Americans only five, with 43 wounded. The Rangers were the only units that found success against Mexican guerilla groups.

Numerous Rangers went with Scott on his march to the interior. Two years prior, Texas ceased to exist as a sole republic and was admitted to the American union as the 28th state. The U.S. took over many matters of military security for the new addition to the union, and the Rangers lost many fine officers to federal service. Recruiting for new members was far below its past levels, as new American regulations stifled enthusiasm for the positions. Ranger companies of the past were amassed and disbanded as needed, but the U.S. Army required enlistment for the entire war.

Nevertheless, Rangers contributed to the fall of Mexico City in September of 1847, signifying the beginning of the end for Santa Anna. His final battle in the war came at Huamantla, a late Texan victory in the struggle. The Battle of Huamantla forced Mexico to lift the siege at Puebla, begun on the same day that Mexico City fell. On October 8, 1847, spies reported that Santa Anna was in Huamantla with a force of 10,000. Samuel Walker arrived, leading a far smaller force of Rangers, and immediately set about attacking a unit of 2,000 Lancers. Santa Anna countered, but was attacked by the main American force. In the melee, Walker was mortally wounded. Following the victory, Major General Joseph Lane heard of Walker's death, and in a fit of anger turned his troops loose on the town of Puebla. The entire community was burned to the ground.

On December 6 of the same year, Hays led his company of Rangers into Mexico City. Despite his legendary reputation, locals often attacked individual Rangers whenever they could find an opportunity. However, the populace soon learned the danger of attacking one of Hays' men. One Ranger took a handful of candy from a vendor, who believed he was being robbed. The vendor threw a stone at the offender and was immediately shot dead. On another occasion, a Ranger shot a pickpocket dead and calmly retrieved his property as if nothing had occurred. Ranger Adam Allsens, caught alone in a dangerous neighborhood of the city called "Cutthroat," was hacked to pieces. His fellow Rangers grieved through the remainder of the day, but by the following morning, 80 bodies lay in the streets of the neighborhood. Seldom was a Texas Ranger ever threatened again. Once Santa Anna was captured and taken back to Veracruz on a safe-conduct pass issued by Scott, security was heightened to protect the Mexican general from Rangers who wanted blood.

An 1840s depiction of the Rangers

Following the Mexican campaign, the Texas Rangers lost their high profile among the public, and like before, were only brought together as a force when needed. However, tensions remained high with Mexico, and Ranger commanders stayed busy with various military units. From time to time, the larger body of Rangers became involved.

The Second Half of the 19th Century

Major John Salmon "Rip" Ford possessed one of the most sterling reputations garnered by a Ranger leader in the Mexican-American War and other engagements. However, many of the most history-making actions in his career would occur between 1858 and the following year. His instructions from Governor Hardin, who also came up with $75,000 of funding, were clear: to "follow any trail and all trails of hostiles…and chastise them if unfriendly."[27] Ford, an aggressive attacker, adopted the nickname of "Rip" for the practice of scrawling "Rest in Peace" by the names of all the enemies killed under his command. He took the broad instructions as license to penetrate deep into the Comancheria, the tribe's stronghold located in what is now northern Texas and central Oklahoma. Throughout the prior year, raids on Texan settlers had increased in frequency and severity, and rumors of a large invasion persisted. Ford intended to put a stop to it in one daring expedition generally referred to as the Battle of Little Robe Creek, on the Canadian River Valley among the Antelope Hills. For his purposes, he brought not only Rangers, but

---

[27] Mike Coppock, HistoryNet, Rip Ford's Risky Ranger Raid – www.historynet.com/rip-fords-risky-rangers-raid.htm

recruited Tonkawas with a reputation for cannibalism.

Ford

In May 1858, Ford's company came upon a small village and attacked it without hesitation. Two Comanche riders escaped and alerted the larger war party, led by Chief Iron Jacket, or Po-bish-e-quash-o. Iron Jacket was famous among his people for possession of a Spanish jacket of mail armor, thought to be impenetrable. As Ford began his attack, a party of over 350 Comanche poured out of the lodges, and a few skirmishes rode into the woods, attempting to entice the Rangers to enter. Ford made it clear that there was nothing for them to fight for in the woods, but since he held Comanche women and children captive, it would be wise for them to come out. Tonkawa were sent in wearing white headbands so that Rangers could tell the difference between friend and foe. However, the headbands were taken off as Comanche marksman could see them as well.

Hesitant to shoot, the Rangers waited as the main body rode out of the woods toward them. Iron Jacket's horse was shot, and he fell to the ground. He was shot twice as he stood to fight and died on the spot. The Comanche, who knew nothing of the Rangers' new Colt weapons and long distance rifles, were stunned at the failure of Iron Jacket's "magic." The battle fell into a series of hand-to-hand encounters covering an area of 18 square miles and raged for at least six hours.

Tonkawa were seen leaving the battlefield with Comanche bodies slung over their horses, many missing feet and hands. These were intended as food to complement the recent buffalo hunt. Despite sensing the advantage, Ford was forced to halt his attack when another large group of Comanche emerged from the hills. The Rangers began an orderly retreat back to Texas after inflicting severe damage, burning lodges as they went.

By the end of 1859, Ford was called again, this time to quell the takeover of the Texas town of Brownsville by the infamous bandit Juan Nepomucenco Cortina. Part raider and part revolutionary, Cortina harbored a special hatred for Brownsville judges and attorneys who he claimed stole land from Mexican Texans. With a large force, he crossed the Rio Grande and subdued the town, camping in the middle of the main street. Ford worked in tandem with then Lieutenant Robert E. Lee, Major Heintzelman, and Lieutenant Fry to force Cortina back to Mexico with artillery and cavalry.

Battles with the Comanche and Texan outlaws continued, but the Texas Rangers of the mid-19th century were falling on hard times in ethical terms. Largely separated from governmental function and often left to their own devices, the next generation of Rangers got involved in many of what would now be labeled as atrocities. Such an example occurred in May of 1860, when Captain "Sul" Ross was called to protect white settlers in and around the present-day town of Margaret. Ross collided with a band of Comanche led by Peter Nocona. In giving his victory an unwarranted importance in the larger picture, he claimed that Nocona was killed and that the Comanche Confederacy was "forever broken."[28] Along with the claim was the sensationalistic headline that Ross's party "rescued" white abductee Cynthia Parker when her blue eyes were revealed. Parker had lived with the Comanche for 34 years and was married to Nocona. In the process, Ross massacred an entire hunting party and their families, and one description suggests that anyone who did not immediately surrender was shot to death without hesitation. Valid arguments were raised in the aftermath as to whether Nocono was present, and many claim he was hunting elsewhere with his son. Ranger Hiram Rogers recounted, "I was in the Pease River fight, but I am not very proud of it…[it was] just a killing of squaws."[29]

Federal soldiers finally gained the upper hand in battles with the Comanche, and the Rangers were disbanded for a time. The problems faced by the new state did not disappear, but the political and social landscapes were changing. Texas became a hotbed of lawlessness committed by its own citizens, both through a dearth of law enforcement apart from the military and because of an embryonic legal code insufficient for the circumstances. Complicating the entire situation was the coming Civil War and secession of Texas from the Union, undertaken only a short time after it had been admitted.

Thousands of Texans found themselves fighting for the Confederacy during the Civil War.

---

[28] Military, Battle of Pease River, www.military.wiki.com/wiki/Battle_of_Pease_River
[29] Military, Battle of Pease River

Even though Jefferson Davis fielded a regiment of Rangers, they were incorporated into elements of the Army and lacked the improvisatory capabilities of their predecessors. One company remained at home, but it fluctuated in size and usefulness, depending on the legislature. Three companies were authorized, but every attempt to fund them failed.

One contrasting example made history through the efforts of Colonel Benjamin Franklin Terry, a wealthy sugar planter who organized his company of Texas Rangers in Houston. Although the company garnered less enduring fame than the Texas Brigade that distinguished itself at Gettysburg, "Terry's Rangers" fought 275 times in four years. They were the only mounted unit to defeat an infantry army, which they did on two occasions. However, Terry led them only in the early weeks before being killed in Woodinville, Kentucky. That tragedy never diminished his reputation, and the company passionately remained Terry's Rangers.

Unlike other units incorporated into the Confederate army, Terry's Rangers were independent to a fault, regardless of orders. Under the official title of the 8th Texas Cavalry, they became infamous for harassing Sherman's march and for defeating the troops of Colonel McCook. In recruiting a distinguished Ranger company of which Terry was never truly a member, the unit's victories were achieved with inexperienced young boys, men well past their prime, and rejects from the Confederacy's conscription.

Closer to home came the formation of the Frontier Regiment, separate from the Confederate Army and assigned the task of protecting the homeland while a large percentage of the men were away. The Texas Mounted Riflemen were installed at the frontier forts, with up to 125 men in each company. Eventually, the cost of maintaining the force overwhelmed the budget, and they were transferred to the Confederacy in 1864.

Much of the progress made in pre-Civil War years to maintain a high degree of performance and integrity among the Ranger companies was thrown into confusion during the post-war Reconstruction. Funding grew so erratic in the years following Appomattox that in a technical sense, official Rangers almost disappeared as an abiding presence during the early 1870s. Still, a few took it upon themselves to organize and act unofficially, but the results often sprang from a sense of vigilantism. What was made official connected the Rangers to the status of 'state police,' an unfortunate and inefficient position for the innovative Rangers to occupy. In the years of Reconstruction, all authority in the South was distrusted and widely despised. The famous names associated with the Rangers began to disappear, and new commanders were "roundly hated"[30] by the same citizens who had hailed their force as heroes only a few years before. Casualties among the Ranger units engaged in the Civil War totaled 483.

---

[30] Mike Cox

A picture of some Rangers in the 1860s

In 1870, Texas was readmitted to the Union, and the regional need for Ranger companies was again apparent. However, unlike the "roughrider" groups of past decades, the modern Ranger acted more often as a lawman than a posse member, making arrests, escorting prisoners from one jail or court to another, guarding jails against illegal mob actions, and attending courts. Texas was changing, and the era of the Wild West outlaw so popularized by modern media was taking shape. Along with the traditional Indian and Mexican incursions, the west experienced the age of the gunfighter. In the following years, Rangers would involve themselves in massive family feuds and pursuit of legendary criminals.

Among the most famous of settler wars was the Horrell-Higgins feud of Lampasas County. The two families were friends and neighbors up to the 1870s, but arguments about property and cattle caused an irreparable rift. The five Horrell brothers ran afoul of the state police in 1873, and Ranger Captain Thomas Williams was sent to the area to address the feud and general lawlessness in the county. Williams fought with the Horrell brothers in Jerry's Saloon, an exchange that left four state policemen dead and the Ranger wounded. Matt Horrell was put in prison, but the brothers broke him out. Gathering a herd of cattle, they disappeared into New Mexico in a racially based killing spree with men, women, and children as victims. All in all, 17 people were killed before the killers returned to Texas, this time as wanted outlaws.

Following Williams' death, Ranger John B. Jones took over. A member of Terry's Rangers, Jones was a slightly built man with a soft-spoken manner. In time, he brokered an agreement between the families, and they signed a treaty. However, two Horrell brothers continued to create trouble elsewhere, possibly killing a store clerk, for which they were gunned down by a vigilante mob. Jones is credited with causing a turning point that helped to end the Indian wars in Texas. In 1874, he led a Ranger company against a large war party of Comanche, Kiowa, and Apache, led by Lone Wolf around Lost Valley. The area was familiarly known as an "Indian death trap,"[31] and the tribes fought hard to preserve the valley, once home to many buffalo. Eventually, they were forced to retreat and abandon their former hunting ground.

A second company of Rangers was created as a counterpart to Jones's Frontier Battalion, called the Washington County Volunteers, or the Special Forces, led by the legendary Leander McNelly. Despite being tubercular, McNelly had a storied career in combat and was responsible for helping to quell the Sutton-Taylor feud and curbing the criminal activity of King Fisher along the Nueces Strip by the border.

---

[31] Texas State Handbook

McNelly

The Suttons and Taylors initiated the bloodiest and longest feud in Texas' history, spanning several years and dozens of lost lives. Many claim that the story begins on a Christmas Eve argument over a sale of horses. However, the first eruptions occurred when former Confederate Buck Taylor killed a black Sergeant who had come to his home for a dance. Similarly, Hays Taylor killed a black soldier in an Indianola saloon. A short time later, two Taylor brothers killed two Yankee soldiers. Among the Sutton family was Deputy Sheriff William Sutton. In one attack, he was wounded when shot through a closed saloon door. Responding, he accompanied a group of Rangers, killing several of the Taylors. In one incident, witnessed by a member of the Taylor family in hiding, Sutton's men arrested two brothers on trivial charges, then took them into the country to gun them down. After 35 lost lives, Rangers were finally able to stop the range war in 1876.

Famed outlaw John Wesley Hardin involved himself in the Sutton-Taylor feud, but he continued his crime spree elsewhere. The son of a preacher, he killed 30 men in his reign of terror, one for simply snoring. Hardin was famous for his "gentlemanly"[32] approach to violence and swore that he had never killed a man who "didn't need killing."[33] A sum of $4,000 was offered for Hardin's arrest. However, the Rangers got there first. Jack Duncan intercepted a letter from Hardin to his father-in-law, revealing his alias and whereabouts as he hid on the Alabama border. Ranger John B. Armstrong inevitably confronted Hardin on a train in Pensacola, Florida in July of 1877, armed with the new Colt .45 revolver. Hardin reached for his gun yelling "Texas, by God!"[34] In a rare misstep, Hardin's gun caught in his suspenders. Instead of shooting Hardin, Armstrong knocked him out and took him into custody. The famous gunslinger became a well-read amateur theologian in prison.

---

[32] Texas State Library and Archives Commission, Rangers and Outlaws – www.tsl.texas.gov/treasures/law/index.html
[33] Texas State Library and Archives Commission
[34] Mike Cox

Hardin

A new type of outlaw arose in Texas as the railroad reached the west coast. Sam Bass created his legend by robbing a Union Pacific train and making off with $65,000 in gold coins and other valuables. A crime binge followed in a series of robberies yielding nothing more than $500. In 1878, he robbed several stagecoaches outside of Dallas, and the Texas Rangers were alerted. Captain Junius Peak, a Kentuckian, Confederate veteran, and member of the Ku Klux Klan, pursued Bass for months, harassing him at every turn in a series of chases and narrow escapes. Betrayed by former gang member, Jim Murphy, Bass was ambushed by Rangers at Round Rock. He survived being shot twice, one bullet striking his gun belt and the other, the stock of his rifle. Inevitably, however, he was mortally wounded and died two days later.

Sam Bass

Leander McNelly, head of the Special Force, confronted many criminal gangs, both Mexican and Texan. Among his accomplishments was to curb the activities of famed rancher and gunman, King Fisher. He recruited 41 men from the Nueces Strip along the border, and the unit became known as the "Little McNellies."[35] McNelly specialized in cattle rustlers and was famous for returning thousands of head back to their original owners. He was also well known for participating in numerous illegal executions, bypassing the courts. He habitually disobeyed direct orders and, despite his many victories, was considered by many to be "too aggressive."[36] King Fisher, a wealthy rancher with an enormous and largely illegal enterprise along the Mexican border, developed into a feared gunman. On one hand a "frontier dandy,"[37] he was a fine horseman and a dead-eye shot with any weapon and with either hand. Commanding great respect in the region, the road to his ranch featured a sign that read, "This is King Fisher's road. Take the other."[38] McNelly kept Fisher at bay for several years by arresting him on a regular basis. During the first altercation, Fisher was prepared to shoot it out with the Rangers. McNelly typically carried a .50-caliber Sharps rifle and the latest Colt revolver, often complaining that the Ranger mounts were better for plowing and that the horse thief Fisher's animals were far superior. Witness Napoleon Augustus Jennings reported that in Fisher's first arrest, in which he intended to shoot it out, he suddenly thought better of it, saying, "I reckon there's too many of yer to tackle...I only wish I'd seen yer sooner."[39] McNelly was never questioned in court about his

[35] Texas Rangers Hall of Fame and Museum
[36] Handbook of the State of Texas
[37] Eyewitness to History
[38] Handbook of the State of Texas

tactics, but tuberculosis forced him into retirement to his farm in the following year. Fisher retired to a quieter, more legal life, at one point serving as a town sheriff. However, he was eventually killed in a gunfight at a Vaudeville theater in San Antonio.

With increasing technology, formal law enforcement, and a general population increase, Texas began to move out of its "Wild West" period in the last quarter of the 19th century, and the Texas Rangers entered their second major era, in which they served as "professional lawmen"[40] in increasingly smaller groups. According to Rip Ford, the disappearing old-time Rangers, 79 of whom were killed in the line of duty in the pre-Civil War years, were generally sober and brave. Newspapers hailed them as "true men, [who] know exactly what they are about."[41] A few reportedly "drank to excess"[42] and were often prone to taking the law into their own hands. However, to the Ranger of post-war years, to do so seemed necessary in light of a weak Reconstruction government. Settlers agreed for the most part, and even the most wayward Rangers were hailed as colorful crusaders led by legendary, bigger-than-life heroes.

The new Rangers who worked into the end of the 19th century and beyond had their share of colorful, extraordinary individuals as well, but for the most part, the units worked within state agencies, and with narrower capabilities for going off on tangents.

John "Turkey Creek Jack" Johnson began his service in Deadwood, South Dakota before relocating to hotspots like Dodge City, Kansas and Tombstone, Arizona to work as a Deputy Marshall with the Earps in 1881. He served in the unit that killed outlaw Frank Stilwell in Tucson. John "Liver-Eating" Johnson, also known as John Garrison, came out of a life in the mountains to serve. The 20th-century movie depicting mountain man Jeremiah Johnson was in part based on Johnson the Ranger. Typical of the new age, Rangers customarily armed themselves with a backup gun, hidden behind the Colt Revolver and called a "belly gun." Surviving the various shootouts the average Ranger was sure to encounter required, in one author's words, a "triumph of instinct over apprehension."[43] The new preference for a backup gun among the Rangers was the No. 2 Ehlers Pocket Model Paterson, a cut-down conversion of the Army Colt .44.

As conflicts with Mexican bandits and native tribes waned, a new threat spread across the ranch and farm lands of Texas, committed by the "night nippers,"[44] who cut barbed wire in the middle of the night. By the 1880s, the frontier was disappearing, and damaged fences meant severe losses for landholders. In 1883, a body of Rangers proposed the installation of bombs at

[39] Eyewitness to History
[40] Harold J. Weiss, Jr.
[41] Texas State Library and Archives
[42] Harold J. Weiss, Jr.
[43] Guns of the Old West, Texas Ranger Backup Guns, December 26, 2014 – www.gunsoftheoldwest.com/2014/12/texas-rangers-backup-guns/#1-/-cad-guns-of-the-gunfighters
[44] Bullock Museum

certain distances apart on fences, designed to explode when cut. A futuristic idea at the time, it was rejected out of hand, so constant patrolling seemed the only alternative. Ranger Ira Aten, however, did not listen and planted numerous charges, refusing to remove them before he had exploded several. Although he did eventually take them out, the rumor spread that every fence in the county was armed with bombs, and the fence-cutting ceased.

John R. Hughes, a rancher, was recommended to the Rangers by Aten after following a fugitive from justice and killing him with a single shot. He later served in the Rangers' D Company. Having no intention of ever becoming a Ranger or joining law enforcement at all, Hughes came to be known as the "Border Boss."[45] His success with the indigenous peoples was due largely to his having lived with various tribes. However, he responded immediately and firmly upon hearing that Captain John B. Jones had been killed in a Mexican ambush. Hughes painstakingly compiled the names of all 18 attackers, hunted them down one by one, and killed them, either by gunfight or hanging.

Regardless of the changing times, colorful standouts continued to join and lead the Rangers. Among the beloved captains of the late 19th century was Bill McDonald, a former penmanship teacher who supplemented his income as a peace officer. He eventually served as a sheriff, a Special Ranger, and as a U.S. Marshall, acting as personal bodyguard to Theodore Roosevelt and Woodrow Wilson. However, what made McDonald so famous was a prize fight he was ordered to stop. The bout between Bob Fitzsimmons and Peter Maher was no ordinary match. At stake was the heavyweight championship of the world. However, the fight was declared illegal, despite McDonald's own Adjutant General and even Judge Roy Bean and Bat Masterson of Western fame being in attendance.

McDonald

[45] Bruce A. Glasrud, Harold J. Weiss, Jr., 4 Dark Days of the Texas Rangers, 1915-1918, Project Muse

Ranger James Brooks attempted to stop the fight, but could not. McDonald arrived in Dallas, where he was met by the mayor, astonished that the Ranger had come alone. Stammering, he is said to have asked where the others might be. McDonald, a legendary marksman answered in a famous quip, "Hell, ain't I enough? There's only one prize fight!"[46]

Officials attempted to move the fight to El Paso and then to Langtry, but McDonald wouldn't have it. The heavyweight championship of the world was eventually fought on a sand bar in the middle of the Rio Grande River. Fitzsimmons won the fight in such fashion that world champion John Corbett immediately announced his retirement. Albert Bigelow Paine's biography on William Jesse McDonald contains an introduction written by an admiring Theodore Roosevelt, and McDonald could count Mark Twain and other celebrities among his friends. The title page of Paine's book declared McDonald's personal creed: "No man in the wrong can stand up against a fellow that's in the right and keeps on a'comin'."[47]

A picture of Rangers at El Paso during the fight

By the end of the 19th century, it was estimated that the Texas Rangers had scouted approximately 173,000 miles and made almost 700 arrests. It is likewise estimated that they returned 2,800 head of cattle to their rightful owners, assisted civil authorities on 162 occasions, and guarded important prisoners in their cells in 13 instances.

A New Century

At the dawn of the 20th century, Texas didn't seem quite sure how to fit the Rangers into the

---

46 Mike Cox
47 Mike Cox

picture, and they were soon perceived as an antique relic of the Wild West. The Frontier Battalion faded along with the frontier itself, and in 1900, a court ruling stripped the Rangers of their authority to make arrests or execute any part of the criminal process. This order all but destroyed the Frontier Battalion and crippled other companies. By 1901, the Frontier Battalion was cut to four companies of 20 men each. These men continued to fight along the southern border as "bloody brush fights"[48] with Mexican nationals continued. Such was the tension along the border that the legislature reconsidered the Ranger question, establishing yet another series of companies in much the same way Stephen Austin had in the early 19th century. The new Rangers were established for "protecting the frontier against marauding or thieving parties"[49] and for the general "suppression of lawlessness." The Frontier Battalion reached new levels of effectiveness in cooperation with a Texas State Police Force, and Captain John B. Jones became Adjutant General of Texas.

In 1906, Bill McDonald returned to Texas, at a time when 167 African American soldiers were falsely accused of causing a race riot and endangering a white woman. All were members of the B, C, and D companies of the 25th U.S. Infantry at Fort Brown. Without identification of any suspects or valid trials, all 167 were removed from the area based on accusations from a citizens' committee. McDonald, described as the Ranger who would "charge Hell with a bucket of water,"[50] pursued the trail of the testimony offered and arrested 12 enlisted men on the charge of "holding positions key to a conspiracy."[51] However, not one was ever indicted or called to testify. Roosevelt dismissed all 167 "without honor,"[52] and that decision would not be reversed until the Nixon administration made things right well over half a century later. McDonald's presence as a single Ranger publicly confirmed the "One riot, one Ranger"[53] motto. It is still inscribed on a statue commemorating the Texas Rangers in Love Field Airport in the region.

The last Wild West-style gunfight occurred in 1904, when Ranger Harry Wheeler, a true gunslinger, shot it out with J.A. Tracy. Both men were shot in the exchange, but Wheeler recovered, and Tracy did not.

A more modern and critical exchange occurred in 1909, when President Taft held a summit with then President of Mexico, Porfirio Diaz, in El Paso. Security was tight. Thousands of troops were present, along with FBI and Secret Service agents and U.S. Marshalls. However, it was Texas Ranger C. R. Moore who discovered and disarmed a man with a hidden palm gun moving only a few feet away from the presidents, intending to kill both.

World War I broke out in 1914, and to the Rangers' tasks was added the identification of spies,

---

[48] Legends of America
[49] Mike Cox
[50] Black Past.org
[51] Texas State Handbook
[52] Texas State Handbook
[53] Military, Texas Ranger Division

conspirators, saboteurs, and draft dodgers. In the following year, a chilling danger faced the southern United States when the Plan of San Diego appeared in the South Texas town. The authorship of the document was unclear, and some have suggested that it was written by the Mexican president himself. The premise of the exhortation was a call for all Chicanos to initiate a racial war, with an invitation added to African Americans, Indians, and Asians. The "revolutionary manifesto"[54] outlined the formation of a "Liberating army of races and people"[55] to free the states of Texas, Colorado, Arizona, New Mexico, and California from control of the United States. This was to be accomplished by murdering every white male over the age of 16, forming a non-white independent republic and annexing it to Mexico. This would recreate the state of Mexican ownership that had prevailed in the previous century. Although the plan was never implemented, its emergence was shocking enough to initiate General Pershing's "punitive expedition"[56] into Mexico. In 1915 and 1916, Mexican raids across the Rio Grande resulted in 21 American deaths, with 300 Mexicans killed in South Texas by vigilantes and private citizens.

In the first two decades of the 20th century, much of the world was occupied with thoughts of exploring exotic climes and celebrating daring heroes. The original Lone Ranger story was penned in 1915 by Western novelist Zane Grey, leading to a proliferation of depictions throughout the century. Experts are adamant that none of these opuses could compare in any way to the true stories of the Rangers, adding that they were a "rag-tag, undisciplined...not always honorable bunch of men."[57] They were farmers and ranchers who wore no shiny badges, carried what 6-shooters were available, and never wore white Stetsons.

In 1916, the equally exotic Pancho Villa raided the town of Columbus, New Mexico, and Rangers serving under Pershing were instructed to keep Mexican raiders out of Texas territory. Considering the violence perpetrated by Villa, a hero to some and a butcher to others, the Rangers reacted in kind. Transforming into an unmonitored vigilante force, they repaid Mexicans with similar atrocities, one so violent that an entire company was dismissed in 1917. Loyal to President Madero, Villa's incursions led to a full-scale battle with the U.S. Army, in which Rangers participated in larger numbers than they had in decades. As a result, Rangers and Special Rangers appointed by the governor participated in the killing of approximately 5,000 Hispanics over the following five years, in keeping with an angry President Wilson's retaliatory mood.

---

[54] Mike Cox
[55] Mike Cox
[56] Black Past.org
[57] Bullock Museum

Pancho Villa

The state government reduced the number of Ranger companies to four, with no more than 17 men in each. A substantial "tightening"[58] of admission requirements was ordered, and guidelines were again put in place. The 35th legislature, contrary to that, created a "Loyalty Ranger Force"[59] under the Hobby Loyalty Act, a secret service organization to the state. Its mission was to brief the Adjutant General on the Mexican activities outside of San Antonio and in the border counties.

The end of World War I came in 1918, and that same year, Prohibition was passed. The Rangers took on the added task of watching for burro trains bringing liquor across the border.

[58] Mike Cox
[59] Mike Cox

Numerous shootouts occurred between Rangers and bootleggers.

The community of Porvenir was the site of the Rangers' greatest atrocity when it came to America's relationship with Mexico. The incident was investigated in 1919 as the worst act of "Ranger misconduct" in the agency's history. A small group of Rangers raided a private ranch, leaving behind 15 dead Mexicans, all residents of Texas. It is alleged that women and children were separated from the men and that all males from teen years to adult were executed. A Mexican adolescent with his arm in a sling was also executed, as the Rangers were searching for a man shot in the hand. Other victims were decapitated, burned, or tortured, with beer bottles shoved into their mouths. Despite the grotesqueness of the scene, it evoked little interest from those living nearby, as the deaths were not American. At the time, the term used suggested that Mexicans were not killed, rather "evaporated."[60] Even scholars such as Walter Prescott Webb, who blames the Mexicans for the incident, agreed that the atrocities committed by Rangers represented an "orgy of bloodshed."[61] The total dead of Porvenir was to grow much higher. Other researchers agree that a "lack of training and controls were evident."[62]

The atrocities did not stop at Porvenir. It was an era in which killing sprees and mass assassinations abounded. Lynchings became common, as did the sight of "bodies flowing down the Rio Grande."[63] According to Hispanics, the Rangers became little more than a terrorist army, and that description was expressed in their common saying, "Rinche, Pinche, Cara de Canche,"[64] translated as "Mean Ranger, face of a bug." The Rangers' worst era was accompanied, not surprisingly for an adoring public, by a sudden "dearth of scholarship."[65] Uneducated readers expected nobility, but actual accounts reported that they behaved, in the words of one author, "with the sensitivity of a rattlesnake."

Again, the Rangers were curbed and overhauled due to increasingly "sordid tales of Ranger brutality."[66] The new world of Texas Rangers that resulted involved a transition to automobiles and a world in which many crimes were committed during the oil boom. Ranger Frank Hamer was the most famous among this group, and did much to restore the organization's reputation. He was almost hounded into joining after apprehending a thief on his own ranch. Hamer rose to the rank of Ranger captain amidst a bank robbery epidemic. The Texas Banker Association offered a $5,000 bounty on robbers, stipulating that in order to receive the reward, the criminal must be dead. Hamer carried a favorite single-action Colt .45 he called Lucky, among many other firearms. Over the course of his career, he survived 50 gunfights.

[60] Tom Dart, Life and Death on the Border: Effects of Century-Old Murders Still Felt in Texas – www.theguardian.com/us-news/2016/jan22/texas-rangers-killings-us-history-life-and-death-on-the-border-mexico
[61] S.E. Spinks, Law on the Last Frontier: Texas Rangers and Their Hell, Review by William D. Carrigan, The Journal of American History, Vol. 95 No. 3 (Dec. 2008)p.864
[62] Tom Dart
[63] Project Muse
[64] Project Muse
[65] Project Muse
[66] Texas State Library and Archives

The most sensationalistic story of the 20th century Rangers took place when Marshall Lee Simmons, head of the prison system, asked Hamer to become special investigator to the case of Bonnie Parker and Clyde Barrow. He traced the murderous couple for over 100 days and led the party that eventually killed them in 1934. More than 130 rounds of ammunition were discharged in the fight.

Hamer

Of the attempts at modern scholarship, Walter Prescott Webb's writings on the Rangers from era to era are considered to be the "beginning, middle, and end of the subject," at least according to Ranger Captain J. Frank Dobie. Despite his "vast array"[67] of factual information, Webb himself graded his own work as merely "a journeyman's job,"[68] greatly preferring his *Story of the Texas Rangers*. Webb earned a degree from UT-Austin in 1915 and later taught in the History department. Twenty years later, his history was out of print, and the plates were bought by the University of Texas. They produced a new edition in 1965. Webb claims that the work took 17 years to write.

In 1968, the Texas Ranger Museum in Waco alongside Interstate 35 was established, featuring

---

[67] Harold J. Weiss, Jr.

[68] Harold J. Weiss, Jr.

numerous artifacts, guns, and memorabilia.

Author Mike Cox, a passionate researcher of Ranger history, attacked revisionists who diminished the band's achievements and asserted that the tangle of the myth is as "closely interwoven as a fine horse hair quilt." [69] He added that the alleged atrocities are "rare and over-exaggerated."[70]

For Hispanics, these paramilitary invaders called Texas Rangers were like the Ku Klux Klan for African Americans. In *Gunpowder Justice: A Reassessment of the Texas Rangers*, Julia Samora paints an entirely different picture, a "systematic refutation"[71] of the glamorized view. The reader is reminded that the Mexicans endured "systematic persecution"[72] and expressed a reality only possible from a victim.

Neutrality in regard to Texas Ranger history is difficult to achieve, so polarizing is the historical experience. The Hispanic view is that Texas and the U.S. stole the land from Mexico. However, others add that Mexico "stole it from Spaniards, who stole it from Indians, who stole it from each other."[73] The American view of Manifest Destiny operated in the same way it did with the native peoples as transplanted Europeans moved West. Land was taken because it could be taken. However, Webb reminds all who study Ranger history to avoid taking the large view in terms of black hats and white hats. To do so, he believes, would "freeze their biographies in time."[74]

Online Resources

Other books about Texas by Charles River Editors

Other books about the Texas Rangers on Amazon

Bibliography

America Remembers, the Texas Ranger Dragoon – www.americaremembers.com/product/the-texas-ranger-dragoon

Biography, Stephen Austin – www.biography.com/people/stephen-austin-37178#1

Black Past.org, Plan of San Diego, 1915 – www.blackpast.org/aaw/plan-san-diego-1915

---

[69] Mike Cox, The Texas Rangers: Wearing the Cinco Peso, 1821-1900, Review by Paul N. Spellman, the *Southwestern Historical Quarterly*, Vol. 113 No. 1, (July 2009) pp. 126-27

[70] Mike Cox

[71] Juian Samora, Joe Bernal, Albert Pena, Review by Larry D. Ball of Gunpowder Justice: A Reassessment of the Texas Rangers. *Western Historical Quarterly*, Vol. 11 no. 2 (Apr., 1980) pp217-218

[72] Julian Samora, Joe Bernal, Albert Pena

[73] Mike Cox

[74] Harold Weiss, Jr.

Bullock Museum, Texas Rangers – www.TheStoryofTexas.com/discover/campfire-stories/texas-ranger

Coppock, Mike, HistoryNet, Rip Ford's Risky Ranger Raid – www.historynet.org/rip-fords-risky-ranger-raid.htm

Cox, Mike, Texas Ranger Hall of Fame and Museum, a Brief History – www.texasranger.org/history/BriefHistory1.htm

Cox, Mike, The Texas Rangers: Wearing the Cinco Peso, 1821-1900, Review by Paul N. Spellman, the *Southwestern Historical Quarterly*, Vol. 113 No. 1 (July, 2009)

Dart, Tom, Life and Death on the Border: Effects of Century-Old Murders Still Felt in Texas – www.theguardian.com/us-news/2016/jan22/texas-rangers-killings-us-mystery-life-and-death-on-the-border-mexico

De Stefano, Rino, La Liguria, June 2002, Captain Jack is the Real Tex Willer – www.rinodestefano.com/en/articles/rangers.php

Eyewitness to History.com, Encounter with the Texas Rangers, 1876 – www.eyewitnesstohistory.com/texasrangers.htm

Glassrudy, Bruce A., Weiss, Harold J., Jr. – 4 Dark Days of the Texas Rangers, 1915-1918

Guns of the Old West, Texas Ranger Back-up Guns, Dec. 26, 2014 – www.gunsoftheOldWest.com/2014/12/texas-ranger-backup-guns/#1-/-ead-guns-of-the-gunfighters

History Lists, 8 Famous Texas Rangers – www.history.com/news/history-lists/8-famous-texas-rangers

Legends of America, Texas Legends, The Texas Rangers – Order Out of Chaos – www.legendsofamerica.com/texas-rangers.html

Lone Star Junction, the Texas Rangers – www.lsjunction.com/facts/rangers/htm

Military, Texas Ranger Division – www.military.wikia.com/wiki/Texas_Ranger_Division

Military, Battle of Pease River – www.military.wikia.com/wiki/Battle_of_Pease_River

Moore, Stephen, Savage Frontier, Volume III, 18401841 – www.untpress.edu/sites/default/files/excerpt/press270.pdf

Parks, Rachel, Fort Hood Sentinel.com, Texas Ranger Museum, Hall of Fame Must See, Sept.

2, 2010 – www.forthoodsentinel.com/texas-ranger-museum-hall-of-fame-a-must-see/article_bc6f0bca-ba7e-5295-8150-4a01e05a5ee0.html

Radu, Alexander, 10 Wild Lawmen of the Old West, List Verse, March 12, 2015 – www.listverse.com/2015/03/12/10-wild-lawmen-of-the-old-west/

Robenalt, Jeffery, Diablos Tejanos: The Texas Rangers and the Road to Mexico, TexasEscapes.com – www.texasescapes.com/Jeffery/Robenalt/Diablos-Tejanos.htm

Samora, Julian, Bernal, Joe, Pena, Albert, Review, Gunpowder Justice: A Reassessment of the Texas Rangers, Review by Larry D. Ball: *Western Historical Quarterly*, Vol. 11 No. 2 (Apr. 1980

Sigurdsson, Sig, Pease River Massacre, Texas Rangers Defeat Comanche, Rescue Cynthia Parker after 25 Years Captivity/Burn Pit, Dec. 19, 2014 – www.burnpit.us/2014/12/pease-river-massacre-texas-rangers-defeat-comanche-rescue-cynthia-parker-after-25-years

Spinks, S.E., Law on the Last Frontier: , Review by William D. Carrigan, the *Journal of American History*, Vol. 95 No. 3, (Dec. 2008)

Texas Ranger Hall of Fame and Museum, William A. Wallace "Bigfoot" – www.texasrangers.org/halloffame/Wallace_William.htm

Texas State Historical Association, Frontier Battalion – www.tshaonline.org/handbook/online/articles/qqf01

Texas State Library and Archives Commission, Rangers and Outlaw – www.tsl.texas.gov/treasures/law/inex.htm

The Texas Ranger Costume – www. – www.CourtBech.com/gstxrangcost1.html

The Texas Rangers and the Mexican Revolution: The Bloodiest Decade, 1910-1920, University of New Mexico Press – www.unmpress.com/books.php?ID=10512063900834

TSHA, Texas State Historical Association, Morrison, Moses – www.tshaonline.org/handbook/online/articles/fmo67

Weiss, Harold, Jr., The Texas Rangers Revisited: Old Themes and New Viewpoints, the *Southwestern Historical Quarterly*, Vol. 97 No. 4, (Jan. 1971)

Williams, R.M. Entry, Biographical Encyclopedia of Texas – www.georgetown-texas-.org/WILLIAMSON_ROBERT_M_Three-Legged-Willie_bio.pdf

Free Books by Charles River Editors

We have brand new titles available for free most days of the week. To see which of our titles are currently free, click on this link.

Discounted Books by Charles River Editors

We have titles at a discount price of just 99 cents everyday. To see which of our titles are currently 99 cents, click on this link.

---

[i] *Criollos*, the Mexican whites, were the children of Spaniards born in America, with no Indian blood.

[ii] The word "Tejas" is not Spanish. It means "friends" in the language of the Caddo nation, which inhabited the area.

Made in the USA
Coppell, TX
17 June 2022